P9-DTQ-608

THE LITTLE

FISH

COOKBOOK

THE LITTLE
FISH
COOKBOOK

SMITHMARK

This edition first published in 1996 by
SMITHMARK Publishers
a division of US Media Holdings Inc.
16 East 32nd Street
New York, NY 10016

Produced by
Anness Publishing Limited
1 Boundary Row
London SE1 8HP

SMITHMARK books are available for bulk purchase for
sales promotion and for premium use. For details write or call
the manager of special sales, SMITHMARK Publishers, a
division of US Media Holdings Inc., 16 East 32nd Street,
New York, NY 10016; (212 532 6600)

ISBN 0-8317-7431-2

Publisher Joanna Lorenz
Senior Cookery Editor Linda Fraser
Assistant Editor Emma Brown
Designers Patrick McLeavey & Jo Brewer
Illustrator Anna Koska
Photographers James Duncan, Amanda Heywood,
Karl Adamson, Steve Baxter & Michelle Garrett
Recipes Carla Capalbo, Steven Wheeler, Christine
France, Carole Clements, Elizabeth Wolf-Cohen,
Hilaire Walden, Sarah Gates, Alex Barker, Liz Trigg,
Shirley Gill & Laura Washburn

10 9 8 7 6 5 4 3 2 1

Printed in Singapore by
Star Standard Industries Pte Ltd

Contents

Introduction

Frequently described as the perfect food, fish is packed with protein, has very little carbohydrate and is a good source of vitamins and minerals. White fish, like cod or haddock, is extremely low in  fat, while the fat in oilier varieties, like mackerel and salmon, is polyunsaturated and highly beneficial because the fatty acids in these fish are believed to play a part in preventing coronary heart disease. If we eat the bones, as we do when we tuck into a portion of pan-fried sardines or canned pilchards, we obtain calcium.

Although healthy eating is a persuasive argument for enjoying fish, it is only one of a raft of reasons. Fish is the ultimate fast food. It is generally sold prepared, needs very little cooking and, because it has less connective tissue than meat, there is very little shrinkage. It is versatile, lending itself to a wide range of cooking methods, such as poaching, steaming, broiling, frying, braising, baking, roasting and even barbecuing. Because of the high moisture content, it is an ideal candidate for the microwave, rewarding the careful cook with maximum flavor. Try it sauced or in salads, with pasta or as the basis for a risotto or pilaf. Stick it on skewers, toss it in a wok with crisp-tender vegetables, try it wrapped in spinach or packaged in paper. Make it into a casserole or a pâté, or enjoy it served simply with a squeeze of lemon juice and grinding of black pepper.

Explore the wealth of different types of fish and shellfish — there are hundreds of varieties and many are seasonal delicacies. Available all year round are cod, flounder, haddock, halibut, herring, mullet, sole, snapper, salmon and tuna.

Choose your market carefully and you shouldn't ever have cause to question the quality of the merchandise. Even so, it is useful to know what to look for when choosing fish. The eyes of whole fish should be clear and bright; the scales or skin shiny and colorful; and the flesh, when you press it, should be firm to the touch. It is sometimes suggested that fresh fish should have no odor, but this is not true: it should have a fresh sea smell; any hint of ammonia (except with skate, which may have a very faint whiff, which will disappear on blanching) and you should certainly not buy. Fish fillets, cutlets and steaks should have

a neat shape; the flesh of white fish should be moist and slightly translucent. If smoked, the fish should have a pleasant smoky aroma and good color. Haddock and herring are usually cold-smoked, and require further cooking, while salmon is usually hot-smoked and so can be eaten without further cooking.

Fish and shellfish (with the occasional exception of octopus) is never tough, but if it is overcooked, the flesh will be dry and tasteless, and nutrients will have been lost. Fish is ready as soon as the protein coagulates. The general advice is to test the fish with the point of a sharp knife; if it flakes easily, it is cooked.

We've trawled the world for the finest fish recipes, from Maryland Crab Cakes to Moroccan Fish Tagine. Within these pages you'll find everything from soups to salads — an irresistible invitation to eat more fish.

7

Familiar Fish & Shellfish

COD

This popular white fish has firm flaky flesh and good flavor. It is good broiled, baked and skewered. Members of the cod family include haddock and pollock. Scrod is a term for cod weighing 2 pounds or under.

CRAB

The meat from this shellfish is of two sorts. Brown meat from inside the hard upper shell is soft and rich, whereas the white meat found in the claws and body is more dense and sweet. Crabs are often sold cooked; choose one that is heavy for its size.

DOVER SOLE

This has long been a favorite, thanks to its delicate flavor and fine white flesh. It is frequently fried or broiled whole.

LOBSTER

The meat of this large crustacean has an exquisite flavor. For best results, buy live lobsters when possible.

MACKEREL

An oily fish that is particularly good broiled or barbecued, mackerel needs a sharp sauce to counteract its rich flavor.

MONKFISH

Ugly to look at but delicious to eat, monkfish has firm, meaty flesh with a flavor reminiscent of lobster.

MUSSELS

Available all year round, mussels have a wonderful, sweet flavor and can be eaten steamed, baked with a stuffing, or added to sauces and salads.

SALMON

Deservedly held in high regard, the fresh fish has firm flesh with a wonderful flavor. Farmed salmon is widely available but the wild fish has an even better flavor. It can be cooked by most methods and is truly delectable poached, baked or barbecued whole. It is also excellent smoked.

SARDINES

Sardines should be eaten very fresh, or cooked from frozen. They can be broiled, barbecued or baked. Canned sardines are a very good kitchen standby and can be used for a tasty pizza topping.

SCALLOPS

The edible part of the scallop is the round white muscle and, if available, the orange, pointed coral, or roe. These tender shellfish are rich yet delicately flavored.

SKATE

Related to the shark, skate is a delicately flavored fish with a cartilaginous skeleton. Usually fried in butter, it can also be broiled or barbecued.

TROUT

More often farmed than wild, trout makes very good gravadlax and is also delicious fried, broiled or smoked.

TUNA

A very large meaty fish, often eaten rare, fresh tuna has a robust flavor. Canned tuna tastes more mellow, and is popular for salads and sauces.

TURBOT

Usually sold as steaks or fillets, turbot is an expensive treat. It has an excellent flavor and is widely considered to be the finest of the flat fish.

Techniques

FILLETING A ROUND FISH

Cut off the head. With the tip of a knife, cut through the skin all along the length of the backbone. Working from head to tail, use short strokes to cut one fillet off the rib bones in one piece. Cut across the tail to release the fillet. Repeat for the other fillet.

FILLETING A FLAT FISH

Make an incision in the skin around the head, then cut down the center of one side of the fish. Working from the head end, and from the center outwards, scrape the flesh off the bones to ease the first fillet away in one piece. Repeat with the remaining three fillets.

SKINNING A WHOLE FLAT FISH

Lay the fish on a flat surface and cut through the skin just above the tail. Ease enough skin away to get a grip, then pull it off. Repeat on the second side. To get a firm grip, you may find it helpful to salt your fingers.

SKINNING A FISH FILLET

Lay the fillet flat, skin-side down, tail end towards you. Cut across the tail end, through to the skin. Grip the bit of skin and insert the knife blade so it is almost parallel to the skin. Cut the fillet away using a sawing motion.

PEELING SHRIMP

Pull off the head, slit or pull the shell apart along the underside between the legs, then use your thumbs to slip it off and release the tail. Straighten the shrimp, then carefully pull out the vein from the head end. If it breaks off, use a sharp knife to make a small cut down the back to remove the rest. Rinse and pat dry.

CLEANING MUSSELS OR CLAMS

Discard any shellfish with cracked or broken shells; also any shells which are not tightly closed or which do not snap shut when tapped. Scrub the shells and remove the hairy "beard" which sticks out from the shell. Rinse under running water. If you have harvested the shellfish yourself, leave them in a large bucket of sea water for several hours, changing the water once or twice, so that they expel any sand. For clams, add a handful or two of cornmeal or flour to the water to help the cleansing process.

SCALING FISH

Holding the fish by the tail under running water over a clean sink, scrape off the scales with a blunt knife. Work from the tail towards the head.

11

COOK'S TIPS

• *To calculate how much fish to buy, the rule of thumb is to allow about 5-6 ounces fish fillets or 6-7 ounces fish steaks per person.*
• *Different types of fish can be mixed in soups and stews to create sensational flavors. Try a mixture of white fish with shrimp.*
• *When poaching whole fish, start with cold water to preserve the shape of the skin; add fillets or steaks to simmering liquid.*

Appetizers

Shrimp & Corn Bisque

INGREDIENTS

2 tablespoons olive oil
1 onion, finely chopped
¼ cup butter or margarine
¼ cup flour
3⅔ cups fish or chicken broth, or clam juice
1 cup milk
6 ounces cooked shrimp, shelled, plus 4 whole shrimp to garnish
1½ cups corn (fresh, frozen or canned)
½ teaspoon finely chopped fresh dill or thyme
pinch of salt
dash of Tabasco sauce
½ cup light cream
dill sprigs, to garnish

SERVES 4

13

1 Heat the oil in a large, heavy-bottomed saucepan. Add the chopped onion, and fry over low heat for 8–10 minutes, until softened.

2 Meanwhile melt the butter or margarine in a separate saucepan. Whisk in the flour, and cook for 1 minute, then gradually pour in the broth or clam juice and milk, whisking until the sauce boils and thickens. Lower the heat, and simmer for about 5–8 minutes, stirring frequently.

3 Add the shrimp to the onion with the corn and dill or thyme. Cook for 2–3 minutes over gentle heat, stirring, then add the sauce, mixing well. Purée 3⅔ cups of the bisque in a blender or food processor, return it to the pan, and stir well. Add salt, and Tabasco to taste.

4 Stir in the cream. Heat the bisque gently, stirring occasionally until warmed through. Do not allow it to approach boiling point. Serve in heated bowls, garnished with dill sprigs and whole shrimp.

Blinis with Smoked Salmon & Dill

INGREDIENTS

1½ cups milk
2 tablespoons butter
1 cup buckwheat flour
1 cup flour
pinch of salt
1 tablespoon fast-rising dried yeast
2 eggs
⅔ cup sour cream
3 tablespoons chopped fresh dill
8 ounces smoked salmon, thinly sliced
dill sprigs, to garnish

SERVES 4

1 Heat the milk with 1 tablespoon of the butter in a saucepan, stirring, until the butter has melted. Pour into a pitcher, and cool to hand-hot.

2 Mix the flours, salt and yeast in a large bowl. Separate one of the eggs. Make a well in the center of the dry ingredients, and add the milk mixture, the whole egg and the extra yolk. Beat to a smooth batter. Cover with plastic wrap, and set aside to rise in a warm place for 1–2 hours.

3 Whisk the egg white in a bowl until stiff peaks form, then fold it into the batter. Heat a heavy-bottomed frying pan or griddle, and grease with some of the remaining butter. Drop tablespoons of the batter onto the pan, placing them well apart. Cook for 40 seconds, until bubbles appear on top.

4 Flip over the blinis, and cook for 30 seconds on the other side. Wrap in foil, and keep hot while cooking the rest, buttering the pan each time.

5 Mix the sour cream and dill in a bowl. Serve the blinis topped with the smoked salmon and dill cream. Garnish with dill sprigs.

14

Crab & Ricotta Tartlets

INGREDIENTS

2 cups flour
pinch of salt
½ cup butter, diced
1 cup ricotta cheese
1 tablespoon grated onion
2 tablespoons freshly grated Parmesan cheese
½ teaspoon mustard powder
2 eggs, plus 1 egg yolk
8 ounces crabmeat
2 tablespoons chopped fresh parsley
½-1 teaspoon anchovy sauce
1-2 teaspoons lemon juice
salt and cayenne pepper
salad leaves, to garnish

SERVES 4

1 Preheat the oven to 400°F. Sift the flour and salt into a bowl, and rub in the butter until the mixture resembles fine bread crumbs. Stir in about 4 tablespoons cold water, and mix to make a firm dough.

2 Turn the dough onto a floured worksurface, and knead lightly. Then roll out, and use to line four 4-inch tartlet pans. Prick the bases with a fork, line with wax paper, and fill with baking beans. Chill for 30 minutes.

3 Bake the pastry shells for 10 minutes, then remove the wax paper and beans, and bake for 10 minutes more.

4 Meanwhile, beat the ricotta cheese, grated onion, Parmesan cheese and mustard powder together until they become soft. Gradually beat in the eggs and egg yolk, then gently stir in the crabmeat and chopped parsley. Add the anchovy sauce, lemon juice, salt and cayenne pepper, to taste.

5 Remove the four tartlet pans from the oven, and turn down the temperature to 350°F. Spoon the filling into the pastry shells, and bake for 20 minutes, until set and golden brown. Serve hot with a garnish of salad leaves.

15

Ceviche

INGREDIENTS

*12 ounces cooked jumbo shrimp, plus 2 extra
to garnish*
12 ounces scallops, shelled, with corals intact
2 tomatoes
1 mango, about 6 ounces
1 red onion, finely chopped
12 ounces salmon fillet
1 red chili
juice of 8 limes
2 tablespoons sugar
2 pink grapefruit
3 oranges
5 limes
salt and ground black pepper

SERVES 6

2 Skin the salmon and cut into small pieces, discarding any bones. Slice the chili in half, and discard the seeds. Chop finely, and add to the mixing bowl. Add

the salmon, lime juice and sugar. Mix gently, cover, and let marinate for 3 hours.

3 Peel and segment all the citrus fruits, except for 1 lime. Drain well, and mix with the fish. Season, and garnish with shrimp and the lime, halved.

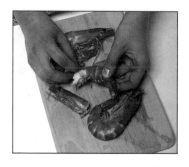

1 Peel and devein the jumbo shrimp, and discard the shells. Using a sharp knife, cut the scallops into ½-inch square pieces. Dice the tomatoes and peel, pit and dice the mango. Place the shrimp, scallops, diced tomatoes and mango in a large mixing bowl. Add the chopped red onion, and mix together well.

16

Broiled Mussels with Cumin

INGREDIENTS

2 tablespoons butter, softened
1 garlic clove, crushed
pinch of ground cumin
3 tablespoons chopped fresh parsley
3 tablespoons chopped fresh cilantro
3 tablespoons fresh brown bread crumbs
12 green mussels or 24 small mussels,
on the half shell
ground black pepper
parsley or cilantro sprigs, to garnish

SERVES 4

17

1 Using a wooden spoon, beat the softened butter with the crushed garlic in a bowl. Add the cumin and the chopped herbs, and mix well. Stir in the fresh bread crumbs, with a generous grinding of black pepper, and mix well to combine. Preheat the broiler.

2 Spoon a little of the bread crumb mixture onto each mussel. Place on a rack over the broiler pan, and broil for 2 minutes. Garnish with sprigs of parsley or cilantro, and serve.

COOK'S TIP

To chop the fresh herbs, either use a mezzaluna (a curved blade with a handle at either end) or simply put the parsley and cilantro in a straight-sided cup, and snip them repeatedly with sharp kitchen scissors.

Maryland Crab Cakes with Tartare Sauce

INGREDIENTS

1½ pounds fresh crabmeat
1 egg, beaten
2 tablespoons mayonnaise
1 tablespoon Worcestershire sauce
1 tablespoon dry sherry
2 tablespoons chopped fresh parsley
1 tablespoon chopped chives or dill
3 tablespoons olive oil
salt and ground black pepper
chives, salad leaves and lemon halves, to garnish
TARTARE SAUCE
1 egg yolk
1 tablespoon white wine vinegar
2 tablespoons Dijon mustard
1 cup corn or peanut oil
2 tablespoons lemon juice
2 scallions, finely chopped
2 tablespoons chopped, drained capers
2 dill pickles, finely chopped
3 tablespoons chopped fresh parsley

SERVES 4

1 Pick over the crabmeat, removing any shell or cartilage, keeping the pieces of crabmeat as large as possible. In a mixing bowl, combine the beaten egg with the mayonnaise, Worcestershire sauce, sherry and herbs. Season with salt and pepper, then gently fold in the crabmeat.

2 Divide the mixture into eight, and gently form each portion into an oval cake. Place between wax paper on a baking sheet. Refrigerate for at least 1 hour.

3 Meanwhile make the sauce. Whisk the egg yolk in a bowl until smooth. Add the vinegar and mustard, with a little salt and pepper, and whisk briefly to blend. Whisking constantly, add the oil in a slow, steady stream until the mixture thickens. Add the remaining ingredients, mixing well. Check the seasoning, cover, and refrigerate.

4 Preheat the broiler. Brush a baking sheet with a little of the olive oil, then carefully transfer the crab cakes to the baking sheet and brush them with the remaining oil. Broil the crab cakes, about 6 inches from the heat, for about 5 minutes on each side. Serve at once, with the tartare sauce, garnished with chives, salad leaves and lemon halves.

Gravadlax Trout

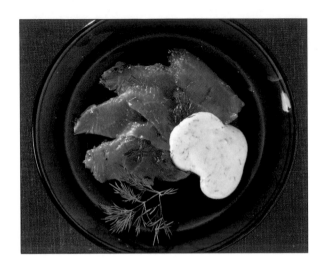

INGREDIENTS

2 large trout, cleaned, heads removed
1 bunch dill
seasonings (see method for quantities): coarse
salt, sugar and black
peppercorns, crushed
MUSTARD SAUCE
1 teaspoon dry mustard
1 tablespoon chopped fresh dill
2 teaspoons sugar
1 teaspoon cider vinegar
5 tablespoons sour cream

SERVES 4

1 Slit each trout from belly to tail in a straight line, open out, and place belly-down on a surface. Press firmly along the backbone, down to the tail. Turn over, and use the point of a knife to ease out the backbone in one piece. Pick out any stray bones.

2 Weigh the trout. For every 1 pound you need 1½ teaspoons each of the seasonings. Place one of the trout in a non-metallic dish, skin-side down. Reserve four dill sprigs for the garnish, and spread the rest on top of the trout to cover it completely.

3 Mix the seasonings, and sprinkle evenly over the dill. Top it with the other trout, skin-side up, cover with foil or a plate, and add weights to compress the fish.

4 Chill for 48 hours, turning every 6–12 hours, and basting with the brine which forms in the dish. Mix all the sauce ingredients together in a bowl, cover, and chill.

5 Remove the dill and seasoning from the fish, and pat dry. Cut the trout into fillets, or slice horizontally. Fan out the slices, garnish with the reserved dill sprigs, and serve with the mustard sauce.

Smoked Salmon Pâté

INGREDIENTS

12 ounces thinly sliced smoked salmon
⅔ cup heavy cream
finely grated rind and juice of 1 lemon
salt and ground black pepper
dill sprigs, to garnish
Melba toast, to serve

SERVES 4

1 Line four small ramekins with plastic wrap. Using a sharp knife, cut the smoked salmon into strips, making sure that the strips are long enough to line the ramekins and overlap the edges. Fit the strips neatly into the ramekins so that there are no gaps.

2 Process the rest of the smoked salmon with the heavy cream and the lemon rind and juice in a food processor or blender until it comes together to give a thick consistency. Scrape the mixture into a bowl. Taste, and add salt and pepper, with more lemon juice, if liked.

3 Pack the lined ramekins with the smoked salmon pâté, then wrap the loose strips of salmon neatly over the top of each ramekin. Cover, and chill for at least 30 minutes before turning out the pâtés onto individual plates. Garnish each plate with dill sprigs, and serve with Melba toast.

21

Lunch & Supper Dishes

Stuffed Sardines

INGREDIENTS

2 pounds fresh sardines, cleaned
4 tablespoons olive oil
1 cup whole wheat bread crumbs
1 onion, finely chopped
⅓ cup golden raisins
½ cup pine nuts
2-ounce can anchovy fillets, drained
4 tablespoons chopped fresh parsley
salt and ground black pepper
banana leaves, to serve (optional)

SERVES 4

1 Preheat the oven to 400°F. Rinse the sardines, and dry them thoroughly with paper towels. Heat about 2 tablespoons of the oil in a frying pan, and fry the bread crumbs until golden. Using a slotted spoon, transfer the bread crumbs to a bowl.

2 Heat half the remaining oil in the frying pan, add the onion, and fry until golden. Stir in the golden raisins, pine nuts, anchovies and parsley. Stir in the bread crumbs, mix well, and add salt and pepper.

3 Stuff each of the cleaned sardines with the anchovy stuffing mixture, taking care to close the cavities firmly. Use a spoon to do this, or your hands if you find it easier. Arrange the sardines close together in a single layer in a shallow ovenproof dish. Sprinkle any remaining filling over the top of the fish.

4 Drizzle the remaining oil over the sardines. Bake for 30 minutes until tender, then serve on banana leaves, if you like.

23

Poached Skate & Black Butter

INGREDIENTS

4 cups water
1 carrot, sliced
1 small onion, sliced
1 bouquet garni
1 teaspoon salt
6 peppercorns
½ cup white wine vinegar
8 skate wings
fresh herbs, to garnish
BLACK BUTTER
½ cup butter
2 tablespoons drained capers

SERVES 4

1 Place the water with the carrot, onion, bouquet garni, salt and peppercorns in a large saucepan. Add 6 tablespoons of the wine vinegar. Bring to a boil, lower the heat, and simmer, uncovered, for 20 minutes. Strain the liquid (court bouillon) into a pitcher, discarding the flavoring ingredients.

2 Rinse the skate wings, and dry them on paper towels. Put them in a large, shallow pan, and cover with the court bouillon. Bring to simmering point, and poach for 10–12 minutes or until cooked. Drain, place on a large platter, and keep hot.

3 Heat the butter in a pan; as soon as it turns a rich brown, remove it from the heat. Stir in the capers. Pour the butter over the skate. Add the remaining vinegar to the pan, and heat through quickly, swirling it around. Pour the vinegar over the fish, and serve at once, garnished with herbs.

Steamed Chili Mussels

INGREDIENTS

2 red chilies
6 ripe tomatoes
2 tablespoons peanut oil
2 garlic cloves, crushed
2 shallots, finely chopped
2½ pounds fresh mussels
2 tablespoons white wine
2 tablespoons chopped fresh parsley, to garnish

SERVES 6

1 Slice the chilies in half, taking care to remove and discard all the seeds. Chop the chilies and the tomatoes coarsely, and place together in a bowl. Heat the oil in a heavy-bottomed saucepan. Add the garlic and shallots, and fry over low heat for 5 minutes or until the shallots have softened. Stir in the tomatoes and chilies, and simmer for 10 minutes.

2 Scrub the mussels carefully, pull off the beards, and discard any which are open. Add with the white wine to the saucepan, then cover tightly, and cook over high heat for about 5 minutes or until almost all the mussels have opened. Discard any mussels that remain closed. Spoon the mussels into a large bowl, sprinkle the parsley over the top, and serve.

Scallop & Mussel Kebabs

INGREDIENTS

3 tablespoons butter, softened
2 tablespoons finely chopped fresh parsley, plus
parsley sprigs to garnish
1 tablespoon lemon juice
32 queen scallops
24 fresh mussels, scrubbed and bearded
8 bacon rashers
1 cup fresh white bread crumbs
¼ cup olive oil
salt and ground black pepper
twists of lemon rind, to garnish
hot toast, to serve

SERVES 8

I Using a wooden spoon, beat the butter with the parsley in a mixing bowl. Gradually beat in the lemon juice, with salt and pepper to taste. Set aside until required. Open the scallops, reserving their liquid in a small saucepan. Cook the scallops in their liquid (or in a little fish broth or white wine) until they begin to shrink. Drain, and pat dry with paper towels.

2 Place the mussels in a large pan. Pour in water to a depth of 1 inch. Cover tightly, and cook for 5–8 minutes until the mussels have opened. Discard any that remain closed. Remove the mussels from their shells, and pat dry on paper towels.

3 You will need eight 6-inch metal or wooden skewers. If using wooden skewers, soak them in water for 30 minutes before use. Pierce a rasher of bacon with one of the skewers, then thread four scallops and three mussels alternately onto the skewer, weaving the bacon in between. Thread the remaining skewers in the same way. Preheat the broiler.

4 Spread out the bread crumbs on a plate. Brush the seafood with olive oil, and roll in the crumbs to coat all over. Broil for 4–5 minutes on each side, until lightly browned. Serve with the toast and flavored butter, garnished with parsley and lemon rind twists.

26

Haddock & Broccoli Chowder

INGREDIENTS

4 scallions, sliced
1 pound potatoes, diced
1 bay leaf
1 ¼ cups fish broth or water
1 ¼ cups skim milk
1 ½ pounds broccoli florets, thawed if frozen
1 pound smoked haddock fillets, skinned
7-ounce can corn, drained
ground black pepper
chopped scallions, to garnish
crusty bread, to serve

SERVES 4

28

1 Place the sliced scallions and the diced potatoes in a large saucepan. Add the bay leaf. Pour over the broth or water and skim milk. Bring the liquid to a boil, then lower the heat, cover the pan tightly, and allow to simmer for 10 minutes.

2 Quarter any large broccoli florets. Cut the haddock into bite-size chunks. Add the broccoli, haddock and corn to the pan, with a generous grinding of black pepper. Cover the pan, and simmer for about 5 minutes or until the fish is cooked through.

3 Remove the bay leaf. Serve the chowder in heated bowls topped with chopped scallions and ground black pepper. Serve with crusty bread.

Quick Seafood Pizza

INGREDIENTS

4 cups white bread flour
1 tablespoon sugar
1 teaspoon fast-rising dried yeast
1 teaspoon sea salt
2 tablespoons olive oil
1¼ cups hand-hot water
TOPPING
1 tablespoon olive oil
1 onion, finely chopped
2 x 14-ounce cans chopped tomatoes
1 tablespoon chopped fresh thyme
8 canned sardines
4 ounces cooked shrimp, peeled and deveined
8 cherry tomatoes, halved
thyme sprigs, to garnish

SERVES 4

1 Sift the flour into a large bowl. Stir in the sugar, yeast and salt. Add the olive oil and water, and mix to a firm dough. Knead on a lightly floured surface for about 10 minutes, until the dough is smooth, elastic and no longer sticky. Return it to the cleaned bowl, cover, and leave in a warm place until the dough has doubled in bulk.

2 For the topping, heat the oil, and fry the onion over low heat for 8–10 minutes, until softened.

3 Stir in the chopped tomatoes and thyme, with plenty of salt and pepper to taste. Simmer, stirring occasionally, for 15 minutes.

4 Preheat the oven to 400°F. Knock back the dough, knead it for 5 minutes, and then cut it into four equal pieces. Roll each piece out to a round, about 8 inches in diameter, then place the rounds on baking sheets.

5 Spread each dough round generously with the tomato sauce, and top with the sardines, shrimp and cherry tomatoes. Bake for 20 minutes until the crust is golden and crisp. Garnish the pizzas with thyme sprigs, and serve.

Broiled Snapper with Hot Mango Salsa

INGREDIENTS

12 ounces new potatoes
3 eggs
4 ounces green beans, ends removed and halved
4 red snapper, about 12 ounces each, cleaned and trimmed
2 tablespoons olive oil
6 ounces mixed lettuce leaves
10-12 cherry tomatoes
salt and ground black pepper
SALSA
1 ripe mango, about 6 ounces
3 tablespoons chopped fresh cilantro
½ red chili, seeded and chopped
1-inch piece fresh ginger, grated
juice of 2 limes
generous pinch of celery salt

SERVES 4

1 Place the potatoes in a large saucepan of salted water. Bring to a boil, then lower the heat, and simmer for 15–20 minutes or until just tender. Drain.

2 Bring a second pan of salted water to a boil. Boil the eggs for 4 minutes, then add the beans, and cook for 6 minutes more, so that the eggs have had a total of 10 minutes. Remove the eggs, and place in a bowl of cold water. Drain the beans, refresh under cold running water, and drain. When the eggs are cold, shell them, and cut into quarters.

3 Make the salsa by processing all the ingredients in a food processor or blender until smooth. Add salt and pepper to taste, and set aside. Preheat the broiler to moderate. Slash each snapper three times on each side, place on the broiler rack, and brush with olive oil. Broil for 12 minutes, turning once.

4 Meanwhile strew the lettuce leaves on four individual plates. Cut the new potatoes and tomatoes in half, and arrange them around the rim of each plate, with the beans and hard-boiled eggs. Center a broiled snapper on each salad, and serve at once, with the salsa.

Salads

Spinach Salad with Bacon & Shrimp

INGREDIENTS

4 ounces fresh young spinach leaves
½ head oak leaf lettuce, coarsely torn
2 tablespoons sherry vinegar
2 garlic cloves, finely chopped
1 teaspoon Dijon mustard
6 tablespoons olive oil
4 ounces rindless streaky bacon rashers,
cut into strips
12 cooked jumbo shrimp,
shelled and deveined
salt and ground black pepper
crusty bread, to serve

SERVES 4

I Arrange all the spinach and oak leaf lettuce leaves neatly on four individual serving plates. Gently heat the vinegar, garlic, mustard and olive oil in a saucepan. Whisk until slightly thickened, and add salt and pepper to taste. Set aside, and keep hot.

2 Gently fry the bacon until the fat runs, then raise the heat, and cook until golden and crisp.

3 Add the jumbo shrimp to the fried bacon, and toss over the heat for a few minutes until they are warmed right through.

4 Spoon the bacon and shrimp onto the lettuce leaves. Add the dressing to the frying pan, and scrape the bottom of the pan with a wooden spoon to incorpo-

rate any bacon bits. Pour a little of the hot dressing over each salad, and serve at once with crusty bread.

Warm Salmon Salad

INGREDIENTS

6 ounces mixed salad leaves (see Cook's Tip)
4 ounces fine green beans, ends removed
3 tablespoons peanut oil
1 pound salmon fillet, skinned and cut into
bite-size pieces
1 tablespoon toasted sesame seeds
DRESSING
grated rind of ½ orange
juice of 1 orange
1 teaspoon Dijon mustard
1 tablespoon chopped fresh tarragon
2 tablespoons sesame oil
salt and ground black pepper

SERVES 4

I Divide all of the mixed salad leaves among four individual serving plates. To make the salad dressing, mix the orange rind and juice, Dijon mustard and chopped tarragon together in a small bowl. Whisk in the sesame oil, and add salt and ground black pepper to taste. Whisk again until all the dressing ingredients are fully combined.

2 Bring a saucepan of salted water to a boil, add the beans, and cook for 5–6 minutes. Meanwhile heat the peanut oil in a frying pan. Fry the salmon pieces for 3–4 minutes until lightly browned. Pour the dressing over the salmon in the pan, and toss gently over the heat for 30 seconds. Remove the pan from the heat.

3 Drain the green beans in a strainer, and arrange them on top of the mixed salad leaves. Spoon the pieces of salmon, together with the hot tarragon and mustard dressing, over the salad. Sprinkle each plate with some sesame seeds, and serve at once.

COOK'S TIP

When time is short, buy a package of mixed salad leaves from the supermarket. Alternatively, put together your own selection, choosing from young spinach leaves, arugula, radicchio, frisée and oak leaf lettuce. Just toss the leaves together.

Melon & Crabmeat Salad

INGREDIENTS

1 pound fresh crabmeat
1½ melons (cantaloupe or small honeydew)
½ cup mayonnaise
4 tablespoons sour cream or plain yogurt
2 tablespoons olive oil
2 tablespoons fresh lemon or lime juice
3 scallions, finely chopped
2 tablespoons chopped fresh cilantro
¼ teaspoon cayenne pepper
3 heads of Belgian endive, trimmed and
separated into leaves
salt and ground black pepper
cilantro sprigs, to garnish

SERVES 6

1 Pick over the crabmeat, removing any shell or cartilage, and discarding it. Try to keep the pieces of crabmeat as large as you possibly can. Using a sharp knife, cut the whole melon in half on a chopping board. Spoon out the seeds from the melon halves, and discard. Then cut the melon into thin slices, and remove the skin.

2 Mix the mayonnaise and sour cream or plain yogurt in a mixing bowl. Beat in the oil and lemon or lime juice, and add the chopped scallions, cilantro and

cayenne, mixing until all the ingredients are well combined. Carefully fold in the crabmeat.

3 Arrange the Belgian endive leaves and melon slices on plates. Spoon a mound of the dressed crabmeat onto each plate. Garnish with cilantro.

Tuna & Bean Salad

INGREDIENTS

2 x 14-ounce cans cannellini or borlotti beans
2 x 7-ounce cans tuna, drained
2 tablespoons lemon juice
1 tablespoon chopped fresh parsley
4 tablespoons extra virgin olive oil
3 scallions, thinly sliced
salt and ground black pepper
Italian parsley sprig, to garnish

SERVES 4–6

3 Whisk together the lemon juice and chopped parsley in a mixing bowl using a small spoon or whisk. Gradually pour in the olive oil, with salt and pepper to taste, whisking all the time until all the ingredients are combined. Pour the dressing over the tuna and beans, and sprinkle with the scallions. Garnish with the parsley sprig, and serve.

1 Drain the beans in a large strainer or colander. Rinse under cold water, and drain again to remove the excess liquid. Stand the strainer or colander over a bowl, and leave for a few minutes, shaking it occasionally, until all the liquid has drained away.

2 Once the beans are as dry as possible, turn them into a serving dish or spread them on a large serving plate. Break the drained tuna into fairly large flakes, and arrange over the beans.

Provençal Salad

INGREDIENTS

8 ounces green beans
1 pound new potatoes, peeled and cut into
1-inch cubes
1 small Romaine or round lettuce, torn into
bite-size pieces
4 plum tomatoes, quartered
1 small cucumber, peeled, seeded and diced
1 green or red bell pepper, thinly sliced
4 hard-boiled eggs, quartered
24 black olives
8-ounce can tuna in brine, drained and flaked
2-ounce can anchovy fillets in olive oil, drained
and torn in half
salt and ground black pepper
basil leaves, to garnish
ANCHOVY VINAIGRETTE
4 teaspoons Dijon mustard
2-ounce can anchovy fillets in olive oil, drained
1 garlic clove, crushed
4 tablespoons lemon juice or white wine vinegar
½ cup sunflower oil
½ cup extra virgin olive oil

SERVES 4–6

1 To make the anchovy vinaigrette, combine the mustard, anchovies and garlic in a bowl or mortar. Mix to a paste by pressing the ingredients against the side of the bowl with a fork or pestle. Season generously with pepper, then whisk in the sunflower oil, then the olive oil, in a steady stream. Whisk until the dressing is smooth and creamy.

2 Bring a saucepan of lightly salted water to a boil, add the beans, and cook for 3 minutes until just tender. Using a slotted spoon, transfer the beans to a colander. Refresh them carefully under cold running water, and drain again.

3 Add the cubed potatoes to the pan of boiling water, lower the heat, and simmer for 10–15 minutes until they are just tender. Drain them thoroughly, and turn into a mixing bowl. Sprinkle with a spoonful of the anchovy vinaigrette.

4 Arrange the lettuce, tomatoes, cucumber, and pepper on a platter. Add the green beans and potatoes, then arrange the eggs, olives, tuna and anchovies on top. Drizzle with the remaining vinaigrette, and serve garnished with basil.

Mixed Seafood Salad

INGREDIENTS

1 small onion, quartered
1 bay leaf
12 ounces prepared small squid
7 ounces raw shrimp, in the shell
1½ pounds fresh mussels, scrubbed and bearded
1 pound fresh small clams, scrubbed
¾ cup white wine
1 fennel bulb
3 tablespoons lemon juice
1 garlic clove, crushed
5 tablespoons extra virgin olive oil
salt and ground black pepper

SERVES 6–8

1 Put the onion and bay leaf in a pan of water. Bring to a boil, drop in the squid, and cook for about 10 minutes. Remove the squid, and slice them into ½-inch rings. Cut each tentacle section in two.

2 Put the shrimp in the pan of boiling water, and cook for 2 minutes or until they turn pink. Drain, and reserve the cooking liquid as the basis for a fish soup, if liked. Rinse the mussels and clams in several changes of cold water, and discard any open shells which do not close when tapped. Place in a large saucepan with the wine. Cover the pan tightly, and cook for 5–8 minutes until most of the shells have opened. Discard any that remain closed. Remove the shellfish with a slotted spoon.

3 Using a small spoon, remove all the clams from their shells, and place in a large serving bowl. Remove the mussels from their shells, and add them to the bowl. Set the fennel fronds aside, then chop the bulb into bite-size pieces. Add to the bowl with the squid and shrimp.

4 Make a dressing by combining the lemon juice and garlic in a small bowl. Whisk in the olive oil, with salt and pepper to taste. Chop some of the fennel fronds finely, and add them to the dressing. Stir, then pour the dressing over the seafood. Garnish with the remaining fennel fronds. Serve at room temperature or lightly chilled.

Mid-week Meals

Moroccan Fish Tagine

INGREDIENTS

2 garlic cloves, crushed
2 tablespoons ground cumin
2 tablespoons paprika
1 small red chili, seeded and finely chopped
2 tablespoons tomato paste
4 tablespoons lemon juice
4 whiting or cod fillets, about 6 ounces each
12 ounces tomatoes, sliced
2 green bell peppers, seeded and thinly sliced
salt and ground black pepper
chopped fresh cilantro or parsley, to garnish
broccoli, to serve

SERVES 4

43

1 In a small bowl, mix the garlic, cumin, paprika, red chili, tomato paste and lemon juice together to form a paste. Arrange the fish in a single layer on a shallow dish, and generously spread the spicy garlic paste over it, using a spoon. Cover, and refrigerate for about 30 minutes to allow the flavors of the paste to penetrate the fish. Meanwhile preheat the oven to 400°F.

2 Arrange half the tomato and pepper slices in a baking dish large enough to hold all of the fish in a single layer. Arrange the fish on top, and cover with the rest of the tomato and pepper slices. Sprinkle with salt and pepper. Cover the dish with foil, and bake for about 45 minutes, or until the fish is tender. Sprinkle with chopped cilantro or parsley, and serve at once, with lightly cooked broccoli.

Halibut with Fresh Tomato & Basil Salsa

INGREDIENTS

4 halibut fillets, about 6 ounces each
3 tablespoons olive oil
basil leaves, to garnish
BASIL SALSA
1 tomato, coarsely chopped
¼ red onion, finely chopped
1 small jalapeno pepper, chopped
2 tablespoons balsamic vinegar
10 large basil leaves, plus extra to garnish
1 tablespoon olive oil
salt and ground black pepper

SERVES 4

44

1 Make the salsa. Mix the tomato, onion, jalapeno pepper and vinegar together in a small bowl. Tear the basil leaves into shreds. Stir them into the salsa with the olive oil. Add salt and pepper to taste, and mix together well. Cover, and allow to marinate in a cool place for at least 3 hours.

2 Preheat the broiler. Brush the halibut fillets generously with olive oil, season with salt and plenty of black pepper, and place on a wire rack over the broiler pan. Cook for about 4 minutes on each side, depending on thickness. Baste the fish with olive oil as necessary. It is cooked when it flakes easily when tested with the tip of a sharp knife. Serve at once, with the salsa, garnished with basil leaves.

Cod & Spinach Packages

INGREDIENTS

*4 pieces of thick cod fillet, about 6 ounces
each, skinned
8 ounces large spinach leaves
1/2 teaspoon grated nutmeg
3 tablespoons white wine
salt and ground black pepper
chopped fresh parsley and lemon wedges,
to garnish*

SERVES 4

I Preheat the oven to 350°F. Season the fish well with salt and some ground black pepper. Bring a large saucepan of water to a boil, add the spinach leaves, and blanch for I minute. Drain, refresh under cold running water, and drain again.

2 Pat the spinach leaves dry on paper towels, then use the leaves to wrap each piece of fish. Sprinkle with nutmeg. Place in a roasting pan, pour over the wine, and bake for 15 minutes. Slice the fish, and serve at once, garnished with the parsley and lemon wedges.

Shrimp Creole

INGREDIENTS

6 tablespoons butter
1 large onion, halved and thinly sliced
1 green bell pepper, halved, seeded and
thinly sliced
2 celery stalks, thinly sliced
2 garlic cloves, thinly sliced
1 bay leaf
2 tablespoons paprika
1 pound tomatoes, peeled and chopped
1 cup tomato juice
4 teaspoons Worcestershire sauce
4-6 dashes of Tabasco sauce
pinch of salt
1½ tablespoons cornstacrh
5 tablespoons water
chopped fresh parsley and shreds of lemon
rind, to garnish
3 pounds raw shrimp, peeled and deveined
boiled rice, to serve

SERVES 6–8

1 Melt 2 tablespoons of the butter in a wide pan. Sauté the onion, pepper, celery, garlic and bay leaf for 1–2 minutes. Add the paprika, tomatoes and tomato juice, then stir in the sauces. Bring to a boil, lower the heat, and simmer, uncovered, until the mixture has reduced by about a quarter, and all of the vegetables have softened. Season with salt.

2 Mix the cornstarch with the water, and add to the tomato sauce. Heat, stirring constantly, until it thickens. Turn the heat down to its lowest setting.

3 Meanwhile melt the remaining butter in a frying pan. Sauté the shrimp, in batches if necessary, for about 2–4 minutes or until pink and tender. When they are all cooked, add them to the sauce. Stir over the heat for about 30 seconds. Check the seasoning.

4 Spoon the rice onto one side of a serving dish, sprinkle the parsley and lemon rind over the top, and fill the remaining space with the shrimp mixture. Serve at once.

46

Spanish Seafood Paella

INGREDIENTS

3 prepared baby squid
8 ounces monkfish or cod fillet, skinned
1 red mullet, filleted and skinned (optional)
4 tablespoons olive oil
1 onion, chopped
3 garlic cloves, finely chopped
1 red bell pepper, seeded and sliced
4 tomatoes, peeled and chopped
1¼ cups arborio rice
2 cups fish broth
⅔ cup white wine
½ cup frozen peas
4-5 saffron strands soaked in 2 tablespoons hot water
4 ounces cooked shrimp, peeled and deveined
8 fresh mussels, scrubbed and bearded
1 tablespoon chopped fresh parsley (optional)
salt and ground black pepper
lemon halves or wedges, to serve

SERVES 4

1 Cut the body of each squid into rings, and chop the tentacles. Cut the monkfish or cod into chunks, and do the same with the red mullet, if using. Heat 2 tablespoons of the oil in a paella pan or large, deep frying pan, add the squid and fish, and stir-fry for 2 minutes. Turn the contents of the pan into a bowl, and set aside.

2 Heat the remaining oil in the pan. Add the onion, garlic and pepper. Fry for 6–7 minutes. Stir in the tomatoes, and fry for 2 minutes, then add the rice, and stir to coat the grains with oil. Cook for 2–3 minutes. Add the fish broth, wine, peas and saffron liquid. Season generously, and mix.

3 Gently stir in the reserved par-cooked squid and fish. Add the shrimp, then push the mussels into the rice. Cover tightly, and cook over gentle heat for about 30 minutes, or until the broth has been absorbed but the mixture is still moist.

4 Keeping the pan tightly closed, remove it from the heat, and set aside to stand for 5 minutes. Check that all the mussels have opened (discard any that remain closed), sprinkle the paella with the parsley, if using, and serve with the lemon.

48

Smoked Trout Pilaf

INGREDIENTS

1 ¼ cups basmati rice
3 tablespoons butter
2 onions, sliced into rings
1 garlic clove, crushed
2 bay leaves
2 whole cloves
2 green cardamom pods
2 cinnamon sticks
1 teaspoon cumin seeds
4 smoked trout fillets, skinned
½ cup slivered almonds, toasted
⅓ cup seedless raisins
*2 tablespoons chopped fresh parsley, plus a few
extra leaves to garnish*
salt
mango chutney and poppadums, to serve

SERVES 4

1 Wash the rice thoroughly in several changes of water. Drain well. Set aside. Melt the butter in a large frying pan, and fry the onion until well browned, stirring frequently. Add the garlic, bay leaves and spices. Stir-fry for 1 minute.

2 Stir the rice into the onion, then add 2½ cups boiling salted water. Bring to a boil, cover the pan tightly, and reduce the heat to low. Cook the rice for 20–25 minutes until tender.

3 Flake all of the smoked trout, and add it to the pan with the almonds, raisins and parsley. Fork through gently, then cover the pan again, and allow the smoked trout to warm through for a few minutes. Serve at once, garnished with the parsley leaves and accompanied by mango chutney and poppadums.

Mediterranean Sole Rolls

INGREDIENTS

6 tablespoons butter
4 sole fillets, about 8 ounces each, skinned
1 small onion, chopped
1 celery stalk, thinly sliced
2 cups fresh white bread crumbs
3-4 drained sun-dried tomatoes in oil, chopped
3 tablespoons chopped fresh parsley, plus extra
to garnish
2 tablespoons pine nuts, toasted
2-ounce can anchovy fillets, drained
and chopped
5 tablespoons fish broth
ground black pepper

SERVES 4

1 Preheat the oven to 350°F. Grease a baking dish with a little of the butter. Cut the sole fillets in half lengthwise to make eight smaller fillets. Melt the remaining butter in a frying pan, and cook the onion and celery over low heat for 15 minutes until softened but not colored.

2 With a wooden spoon, mix the bread crumbs, sun-dried tomatoes, parsley, pine nuts, and the anchovies together in a large mixing bowl. Stir in the softened vegetables with the pan juices. Mix together until combined. Season with pepper.

3 Divide the stuffing into eight equal portions, and roll each one into a ball. Place each stuffing ball at one end of a sole fillet, and roll up. Secure the rolls with individual toothpicks.

4 Arrange all the sole rolls in the prepared baking dish. Pour over the broth, and cover the dish with a piece of buttered foil. Bake for about 20 minutes or until the fish flakes easily when tested with the point of a sharp knife. Remove all of the toothpicks, and sprinkle the fish with chopped parsley. When serving the sole rolls, drizzle a little of the cooking juices over each portion.

Mackerel Kebabs with Parsley Dressing

INGREDIENTS

1 pound mackerel fillets
finely grated rind and juice of 1 lemon
3 tablespoons chopped fresh parsley
16 cherry tomatoes
8 pitted black olives
salt and ground black pepper
chopped fresh parsley, to garnish
mixed salad leaves (optional) and
boiled rice or noodles, to serve

SERVES 4

1 Cut the fish into 1 1/2-inch chunks, and place in a bowl. Add half the lemon rind and juice, half the parsley and a sprinkling of salt and pepper. Stir to mix, then cover the bowl, and leave in a cool place to marinate for 30 minutes. Preheat the broiler.

2 You will need eight 6-inch metal or wooden skewers. If using wooden skewers, soak them in water for 30 minutes before use. Drain the fish, discard the marinade, and thread the chunks alternately with the tomatoes and olives on the skewers. Broil the kebabs for 3–4 minutes, turning occasionally, until the fish is cooked through.

3 In a bowl, mix the remaining lemon rind and juice with the rest of the parsley. Add salt and pepper to taste. Serve the kebabs on a bed of rice or noodles, drizzle with the dressing, and sprinkle with chopped parsley. Add a salad garnish, if liked.

Golden Fish Pie

INGREDIENTS

1 ½ pounds white fish fillets
1 ¼ cups milk
1 bay leaf
1 teaspoon black peppercorns
½ onion, sliced
4 ounces cooked shrimp, peeled and deveined
½ cup butter
½ cup flour
1 ¼ cups light cream
3 ounces Swiss cheese, grated
*1 bunch watercress, leaves stripped from
stems, chopped*
1 teaspoon Dijon mustard
5 sheets filo pastry
salt and ground black pepper

SERVES 4–6

1 Place the fish fillets in a large saucepan. Pour over the milk, and add the bay leaf, peppercorns and onion slices. Bring to a boil, lower the heat, cover, and simmer for 10–12 minutes, until the fish is almost tender. Do not allow it to overcook.

2 Drain the fish, reserving the milk. Remove the skin and bones, then flake it coarsely into a shallow pie dish. Scatter the shrimp over the top.

3 Melt ¼ cup of the butter in a pan. Stir in the flour, and cook for about 1 minute, then stir in the reserved milk and cream. Bring to a boil, stirring constantly, then lower the heat, and simmer for 2–3 minutes, until the sauce thickens.

4 Remove the pan from the heat, and stir in the cheese, watercress and mustard, with salt and pepper to taste. Pour over the fish, and let cool.

5 Preheat the oven to 375°F. Melt the remaining butter. Brush one sheet of the filo pastry with a little of the butter, then crumple it up loosely, and place on top of the filling. Repeat with the rest of the filo and butter, to cover the fish. Bake for 25–30 minutes, until crisp and golden.

Dinner
Party Dishes

Salmon with Herb Butter

INGREDIENTS

1/4 cup butter, softened
finely grated rind of 1/2 small lemon
1 tablespoon lemon juice
1 tablespoon chopped fresh dill
4 salmon steaks
2 lemon slices, halved
4 dill sprigs
salt and ground black pepper
new potatoes and salad, to serve

SERVES 4

3 Cut the frozen butter into eight rounds. Place two rounds in the center of each salmon steak, with half a lemon slice and a dill sprig on top. Close up the foil neatly around the salmon pieces, making sure each package is well sealed.

4 Bake the salmon for 20 minutes. Test by partially opening a package, and piercing the salmon with a sharp knife; the flesh should flake easily. Serve the packages with new potatoes and salad.

55

1 Mix together the butter, lemon rind and juice. Add the dill, with seasoning to taste, and mix well. Spoon onto a piece of wax paper, and roll up, smoothing with your hands to make a sausage shape. Twist the ends tightly, roll in plastic wrap, and freeze the package for 20 minutes, or until firm.

2 Preheat the oven to 375°F. Cut out four squares of foil, each large enough to enclose a salmon steak. Grease the squares lightly, and center a salmon steak on each one.

Spanish-style Hake

INGREDIENTS

2 tablespoons olive oil
2 tablespoons butter
1 onion, chopped
3 garlic cloves, crushed
1 tablespoon flour
½ teaspoon paprika
4 hake or haddock cutlets, about 6 ounces each
8 ounces fine green beans, ends removed
and cut into 1-inch lengths
1½ cups fish broth
⅔ cup dry white wine
2 tablespoons dry sherry
16-20 fresh mussels, scrubbed and bearded
3 tablespoons chopped fresh parsley
salt and ground black pepper
crusty bread, to serve

SERVES 4

1 Heat the oil and butter in a large frying pan. Add the onion, and cook for 5 minutes over moderate heat, until softened but not browned. Stir in the crushed garlic, and cook for 1 minute more.

2 Mix the flour and paprika in a shallow bowl. Lightly dust the fish cutlets with the mixture. Push the onion and garlic to one side of the frying pan, add the fish, and fry until golden on both sides.

3 Stir in the beans, broth, wine and sherry. Season, then bring to a boil, and cook for 2 minutes.

4 Add the mussels and parsley to the pan, cover tightly, and cook for 5–8 minutes or until the mussels have opened. Discard any that remain closed. Divide among heated, shallow soup bowls, sprinkle with pepper, and serve with plenty of crusty bread.

Trout with Hazelnuts

INGREDIENTS

½ cup hazelnuts
5 tablespoons butter
4 trout, about 10 ounces each
2 tablespoons lemon juice
salt and ground black pepper
2 lemon slices, quartered, and Italian parsley
sprigs, to garnish

SERVES 4

1 Preheat the broiler. Spread out the nuts in a single layer in a broiler pan. Toast the nuts, shaking the pan frequently, until the skins split. Turn the nuts onto a clean dish towel, and rub off the skins. Let the nuts cool, then chop them coarsely.

2 Heat ¼ cup of the butter in a large frying pan. Season the trout inside and out, and then fry them, in batches if necessary, for 12–15 minutes, turning once, until the skins are brown and the flesh flakes easily when tested with the point of a sharp knife. Drain on paper towels, before transferring to a platter and keeping hot.

3 Melt the rest of the butter in the frying pan, and fry the hazelnuts until evenly browned. With a wooden spoon, stir the lemon juice into the pan, and mix

well, then quickly pour the buttery hazelnut sauce over the trout. Serve the trout at once, garnished with the lemon and parsley sprigs.

57

Monkfish, Salmon & Sole Mousseline

INGREDIENTS

8 ounces monkfish, removed from the bone
8 ounces sole fillets
2 egg whites
1/2 teaspoon grated nutmeg
1 cup heavy cream
8 large spinach leaves
12 ounces salmon fillet
1 pound tomatoes
salt and ground black pepper
dill sprigs, to garnish

SERVES 4

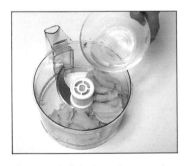

I Line four small ramekins with wax paper. Remove the membrane from the monkfish, if necessary, by cutting it away with a sharp knife and pulling it off. Cut the monkfish into large cubes, and place in a food processor or blender. Skin the sole fillets, and chop into several large pieces, removing any stray bones. Add to the monkfish, with the egg whites, and process until the mixture is smooth and firm. Scrape into a mixing bowl, and refrigerate for 10 minutes.

2 Stir the nutmeg into the mixture, and season. Place the bowl over a second bowl filled with ice. Gradually beat in the cream, then chill the mousseline for 30 minutes, by which time it should be thick and firm enough to hold its own shape.

3 Preheat the oven to 350°F. Blanch the spinach leaves briefly in boiling water, then drain, refresh under cold water, and drain again. Cut the salmon into eight slices. Line the base of each ramekin with a slice of salmon, top with a spinach leaf, cut to fit, add a layer of the mousseline, then add a second spinach leaf, cut to fit. Spoon more mousseline on top, and finish with a layer of salmon. Cover each ramekin with a round of wax paper.

4 Place the ramekins in a large roasting pan, pour in boiling water to come halfway up the ramekins, and bake for 20 minutes. Meanwhile make the sauce. Broil the tomatoes until the skins are blackened. Scrape the flesh into a food processor or blender, add plenty of salt and pepper, and process to a purée. Invert the fish and mousseline molds on individual dishes, garnish with dill, and serve with the tomato sauce.

Tuna with Pan-fried Tomatoes

INGREDIENTS

4 tuna steaks, about 6 ounces each
2-ounce can anchovy fillets, drained
and chopped
3 garlic cloves, chopped
¾ cup olive oil
4 tablespoons lemon juice
1½ teaspoons chopped fresh thyme
12 ounces plum tomatoes, halved
3 tablespoons chopped fresh parsley
8-12 black olives, pitted and chopped
ground black pepper
crusty bread, to serve

SERVES 4

I Place the tuna steaks in a shallow, non-metallic dish which is just large enough to hold them side by side. Place the anchovy fillets and garlic in a mixing bowl, then stir in 4 tablespoons of the oil. Add the lemon juice, thyme and a generous grinding of black pepper. Mix well, pour the mixture over the tuna, cover, and allow to marinate for at least 1 hour.

2 Preheat the broiler. Drain the tuna, reserving the marinade, and place on the broiler rack. Broil for about 4 minutes on each side, basting frequently with the reserved marinade. The tuna steaks should not be overcooked, and are ready when the flesh feels firm to the touch.

3 Meanwhile heat the remaining oil in a frying pan. Add the tomatoes, and fry for 2 minutes only on each side. Divide the tomatoes between four heated serving plates, and sprinkle over the chopped parsley and olives. Top each portion with a tuna steak.

4 Add the remaining marinade to the pan juices, and heat through. Pour over the tomatoes and tuna steaks, and serve at once, with crusty bread for mopping up the juices.

Pan-fried Sole

INGREDIENTS

4 Dover sole or lemon sole fillets,
about 1½ pounds, skinned
¾ cup milk
¾ cup flour
2 tablespoons corn oil
2 tablespoons butter
2 tablespoons chopped fresh parsley
salt and ground black pepper
lemon wedges, to serve

SERVES 4

61

I Rinse the Dover or lemon sole fillets, and pat them dry with paper towels. Pour the milk into a shallow baking dish, large enough to hold a fish fillet. Spread out the flour in a second shallow dish, and season it lightly with salt and pepper.

2 Heat the oil and butter in a large frying pan (big enough to hold two fillets without breaking them) over moderately high heat. Dip each fish fillet in milk, then in flour, turning until well coated. Shake off the excess flour.

3 Add two fish fillets to the hot oil in the frying pan. Reduce the heat slightly, and cook the fish fillets for 3–4 minutes, or until lightly browned, turning once. Remove, and keep hot while cooking the remaining fish fillets. Sprinkle the fish with chopped parsley, and serve with lemon wedges.

Lobster Thermidor

INGREDIENTS

2 live lobsters, about 1½ pounds each
1½ tablespoons butter
2 tablespoons flour
2 tablespoons brandy
½ cup milk
6 tablespoons whipping cream
1 tablespoon Dijon mustard
lemon juice (see method)
grated Parmesan cheese, for sprinkling
salt and white pepper
parsley and dill sprigs, to garnish
French bread, to serve

SERVES 2–4

1 Bring a large saucepan of salted water to a boil. Put the lobsters in head first, cover, and cook them for 8–10 minutes or until bright pink. Remove from the pan and cut in half lengthwise. Discard the dark sac behind the eyes, then pull out the string-like intestine from the tail. Remove the meat from the shells, reserving the coral and liver, rinse the shells, and wipe dry. Cut the meat into bite-size pieces.

2 Melt the butter in a heavy-bottomed saucepan. Stir in the flour, and cook for 1 minute, then pour in the brandy and milk, whisking constantly until smooth. Whisk in the cream and mustard.

3 Press the lobster coral and liver through a strainer into the sauce. Whisk very well. Reduce the heat to low, and simmer the sauce gently for about 10 minutes, stirring frequently, until it thickens. Stir in lemon juice and seasoning to taste (it may not be necessary to add salt).

4 Preheat the broiler. Arrange the lobster shells in a shallow, flameproof baking dish. Stir the lobster meat into the sauce, and divide the mixture evenly between the shells. Sprinkle lightly with Parmesan, and broil until golden. Garnish with parsley and dill, and serve at once with French bread.

Index